THE M
OF ATT   ON

BY MARLANE GOMARD MEYER

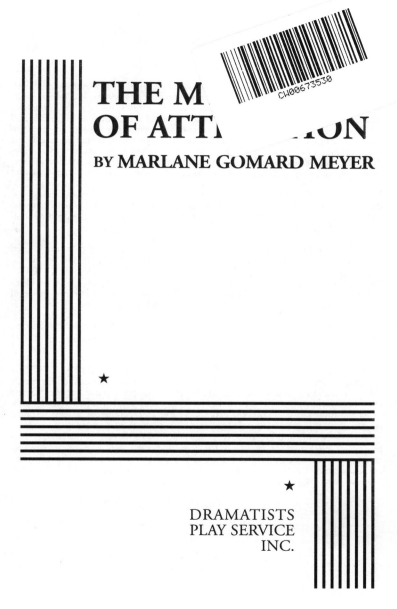

DRAMATISTS
PLAY SERVICE
INC.

THE MYSTERY OF ATTRACTION
Copyright © 2003, Marlane Gomard Meyer

All Rights Reserved

SPECIAL NOTE

Commissioned by the Audrey Skirball Kenis Foundation.

World premiere in the 2002 Humana Festival of New American Plays
at Actors Theatre of Louisville.

The New York premiere was produced by Carol R. Fineman
and The Worth Street Theater Company.

THE MYSTERY OF ATTRACTION was originally produced in the 2002 Humana Festival of New American Plays at Actors Theatre of Louisville.

The New York premiere of THE MYSTERY OF ATTRACTION was produced by Carol R. Fineman and The Worth Street Theater Company at The Tribeca Playhouse, opening on January 12, 2003. It was directed by Jeff Cohen; the set design was by Marion Williams; the lighting design was by Mary-Louise Geiger; the sound design was by Paul Adams; the costume design was by Veronica Worts; and the production stage manager was Michal V. Mendelson. The cast was as follows:

ROGER .... Dan Ahearn
RAY .... Richard Bekins
VICKIE .... Kendra Leigh Landon
WARREN .... Barry Del Sherman
LARRY .... Jefferson Slinkard
DENISE .... Deirdre O'Connell

CHARACTERS

RAY, a lawyer in his forties, alert, damaged, cerebral, cautious, cunning and ultimately unlucky, but with no sense of defeat.

WARREN, Ray's brother, a policeman in his late thirties. He's intelligent and open; he projects a sense of innocence and experience by turns.

DENISE, Ray's wife, forties, resilient but not hard. A good listener, a survivor.

ROGER, a wealthy businessman, patient and loving but clearly a businessman.

LARRY, an enforcer, not conventional, more like a visitor from another planet, enjoys his work but displays little or no emotion.

VICKIE, a very pretty female psychotic.

PLACE

The living room of Ray's home in Torrance, a suburb of Los Angeles. It is a little after 11:00 P.M.

TIME

The present.

THE MYSTERY
OF ATTRACTION

Eleven o'clock at night. A sparsely furnished living room; couch, two chairs, coffee table, lamps. An exterior door can be seen down right. Two interior doors can be seen at either side of the stage. A bottle of Scotch, an ice bucket and two glasses can be seen on a small side table, down right. The entire upstage wall is glass with sliding doors, behind which can be seen a beautiful tropical garden. It is lit for night viewing with Malibu lights. Vicky stands upstage, facing out, staring out. Ray and Roger stand downstage, left and right, at either side, facing up. They watch her.

ROGER. She's like a daughter to me, but she's not my daughter, she's my fourth wife's daughter. I raised her after the wife was killed in an avalanche. She is nothing like the mother, the mother was a monster. But the girl is sweet, docile. For years such an idyllic relationship exists between us that I'm on the verge of taking her as my bride when suddenly she is always in trouble. Escalating calamity as she matures. Disappearing every other weekend, lowlifes shaking me down, shoplifting, drug abuse and a string of accidental homicides. *(Ray looks at Roger.)* She says accidental and I believe her.
RAY. Who did she kill?
ROGER. Let's talk about who she killed this time.
RAY. Okay.
ROGER. Let me first say this. I've spent a lot of money keeping her out of jail. But does she appreciate it? No. She sees life as an experiment. A series of adventures. So this time, she confesses. *(He watches her.)* She wanted to see, from the inside, how the justice system works. So, she confessed. The cops have the knife. Her

5

prints are on the knife.

RAY. Who did she kill?

ROGER. I think she's doing it to spite me. That's right, isn't it? *(Vicky ignores him.)* She's in a rebellious phase ... Who did she kill? This guy named Vince, ex-fighter, stuntman, loser, doper ... They came to the house in Palos Verdes one time and when they left so did the silver. I'm talking sterling, at least twenty thousand dollars worth of sterling and you know what they did with it? They sold it at a swap meet out of the trunk of their car. A dollar a spoon, a dollar a fork. For sterling. What are you gonna do with a kid like that?

RAY. How about lock her up?

ROGER. For stealing silverware?

RAY. For murder? I'm saying that maybe it's right your daughter do time. Time is not the worst thing that can happen to a person who is testing the limits of morality.

ROGER. For one thing I no longer think of her as my daughter, I think of her as my fiancée. And the second thing is the penal system is a whorehouse. Guards sexually abuse the females under their protection on a regular basis. Don't you read the newspaper?

RAY. No.

ROGER. You don't read a paper?

RAY. I don't need a newspaper to tell me that evil flourishes, all I have to do is wake up, stay here, and people like you come to see me.

ROGER. My object in coming here is to see that she keeps from slipping through the cracks.

RAY. I understand that.

ROGER. But also that she gets the help she needs.

RAY. Okay.

ROGER. Because I don't want you to think for a moment there won't be retribution, just not at the hands of the state.

RAY. The law should be the same for everyone.

ROGER. But it's not.

RAY. I think the best thing you can do is to let discipline be administered. Bad dog.

ROGER. That's not why I'm here. Counselor. That's not what's happening here. Discipline the dog. She is not a dog, she's a delicious gumdrop. She kills zeroids. Nobody ever wonders what happened to them. Nobody ever publishes an article questioning what happened to all the John Does. Okay, granted, she might have problems with socialization. But she's my responsibility and I love her and I have to do everything I can for her.

RAY. I'm giving you my best advice.

ROGER. I think you're trying to shake me down.

RAY. Not at all.

ROGER. Because I have a lot of money.

RAY. I said when you called I didn't know if I could help you or not.

ROGER. Look. The situation is that when she goes to trial I want her to get off. Can this be done?

RAY. This is America and there are two types of justice, one for the rich and one for the poor. Which are you?

ROGER. What do you think?

RAY. Then it can be done.

ROGER. Are you the man to do it?

RAY. No, I am not.

ROGER. I know you have connections in the system.

RAY. I don't know what you're talking about.

ROGER. I happen to know you need money.

RAY. Anybody who looks at my shoe leather knows that.

ROGER. I also know you have a problem.

RAY. A man without a problem is not a man.

ROGER. You are in trouble with the animals and the animals are about to open you up and take a piece out.

RAY. But nobody knows which piece.

ROGER. I do.

RAY. *(Shaken, he laughs.)* You know which piece? Really ... you know which piece they're taking?

ROGER. Do you have children?

RAY. Supposedly, I have a daughter in Phoenix I've never seen.

ROGER. Well, at least you'll have the one child then.

RAY. *(He lets it sink in.)* So you're saying they're going to ... *(Beat.)* They wouldn't do that.

ROGER. Oh really...?

RAY. It's a shitty little twenty grand note!

ROGER. Getting bigger every day you don't pay.

RAY. Look, let's ... you go, please ... I don't want to be rude but, this is ... good night.

ROGER. Ray, may I call you Ray? Ray, you seem more concerned about doing the right thing than saving your own dick.

RAY. Roger, may I call you Roger? Roger, I believe there is a balance and order in the world that we will all have to reclaim for ourselves one day, and Roger, if that is indeed your name? Today is my day. Good night. *(Roger takes out his checkbook and tears off a check, leaves it on the coffee table.)*

ROGER. I'm leaving you a check for the amount of your debt.

RAY. I wish you wouldn't.

ROGER. And then some. If you cash it, and I'm assuming you will, then you'll handle our problem. If you don't ... Well, I can only assume you're not as bright as you seem. *(Exiting.)* Victoria, come. *(Vicky moves toward Ray, watches him, moving closer, menacing, smiling ...)* Vicky! Leave him alone. *(Vicky exits. Ray locks up for the night. He looks at the check. He can't bring himself to tear it up. He hides it. Turns off the interior lights. He moves to the garden window, looks out at the garden, a moment of appreciation before he turns off the lights outside. A moment, he turns the lights back on, and his brother Warren appears. Ray opens the door.)*

WARREN. Hi.

RAY. How long have you been out there?

WARREN. I saw that you had company and I just waited out here.

RAY. Come in.

WARREN. What time is Denise home?

RAY. It's her late night. *(Warren enters. An awkward moment.)*

WARREN. You want a drink?

RAY. I was going to bed.

WARREN. Uh, if you want to go to bed we'll just make it a short one. *(Warren pours them both a drink.)*

RAY. I thought you were off the sauce.

WARREN. I am, I'm quit, just, you know, now and then.

RAY. Me, too. *(They drink.)*

WARREN. So. Who's this guy?

RAY. He's a client, was going to be, maybe but ... not my kinda thing.

WARREN. What's he doing here at the house in the middle of the night?

8

RAY. Well ... *(Beat.)* I had to let go of my office and I was busy all day doing fuck-all ...

WARREN. You let go of the office?

RAY. Don't tell Denise.

WARREN. Okay.

RAY. *(Changing the subject.)* So. What's up, bro?!

WARREN. Nothing, you know ... I just dropped by. Haven't been by in a while, in the neighborhood and saw your lights.

RAY. In the neighborhood. You live in Marina Del Rey, I live in Torrance.

WARREN. Ray? Do you think there's something wrong with me?

RAY. *(A moment.)* Yes.

WARREN. Really?

RAY. Yes.

WARREN. Because I don't remember there always being something wrong with me but NOW there is. You know? Before I was married I didn't think about myself the way I do now. I think about myself all the time now. And I think there's something wrong.

RAY. Why don't you go home and talk this over with Sharky?

WARREN. She started all this and now she doesn't want listen to me anymore. She tells me to put a lid on it.

RAY. Are you two fighting again?

WARREN. If my heart is breaking open and the words are coming out all I want is to be held ... to be held and reassured, not told that I'm a mama's boy or that I have a Peter Pan complex. And what's wrong with having a Peter Pan complex anyway? Who doesn't want to sail away to Never-Never Land and have Wendy take care of the details?

RAY. It's the Wendys of the world who write those books.

WARREN. The point is, I don't want to be fixed.

RAY. Then you shouldn't be married.

WARREN. I never thought there was anything wrong with me and now I don't trust myself anymore, I find myself lying to retain my privacy, I don't like to lie.

RAY. It's not a perfect world, but there are trade-offs, unnegotiated trade-offs we silently assent to.

WARREN. Like what?

RAY. How about cooking?

9

WARREN. I do all the cooking.

RAY. What about the shopping?

WARREN. Since I cook I do the shopping.

RAY. Cleaning up?

WARREN. She never does any of that for me and you left out sex.

RAY. I don't like to think about you and Sharky having sex.

WARREN. We don't have sex anymore, Ray, why is that?

RAY. Jesus, Warren, I don't know.

WARREN. Have you ever hit your wife?

RAY. No! *(Ray pours himself another drink.)* I am not a caveman. I have cultivated myself, I have cultivated my responses. I'm a civilizing influence, and to be that you must be civilized.

WARREN. Uh huh ...

RAY. Stuff like wife-beating only happens at night. You shouldn't stay up so late.

WARREN. Up late is the problem.

RAY. For some.

WARREN. Don't you think that at this point in time men and women should be able to talk to each other? But we can't because women don't listen.

RAY. No, they are listening, they are listening for a way to present their agenda.

WARREN. Which is to fix what's wrong with you.

RAY. That's not all women. Some women, well, they have a life.

WARREN. A life of the mind?

RAY. Sometimes, yes.

WARREN. We're not attracted to those women.

RAY. Yes, we are.

WARREN. No, we're old now ... and we can be honest. That type of woman scares us.

RAY. I've dated women lawyers that were ...

WARREN. Very smart and you dated them a few times and you took them to bed but it didn't last because you couldn't relax.

RAY. What, are you in my head?

WARREN. Tell me I'm wrong.

RAY. The chemistry was off. This was right after the divorce and I was having a hard time relaxing with anyone.

WARREN. Shit.

RAY. I think we both pick bright women.

WARREN. But we don't think they're brighter than we are until it's too late. We think we have the upper hand, they let it happen, they let us believe in our superiority, and then wham ... one day you're going through the mail and you find the Mensa newsletter.

RAY. What are you talking about, Sharky's been a member of Mensa for years, she never goes to the meetings.

WARREN. I never knew that.

RAY. What difference does it make?

WARREN. It's huge. Knowing she's got these ... I.Q. Points makes me feel like I have to answer all her questions. And when I do, she analyzes everything I say. But more than that, she analyzes everything I DON'T say, I mean, who cares what it means when you're late AGAIN.

RAY. So you were late again?

WARREN. I don't have to be anybody's boy on time!

RAY. You know you should call.

WARREN. You know, Ray, when God invented woman he did not say I am making you an equal, he said I am making you a help-mate. But like most men he's not listening because Eve's wearing not a stitch so he's in a fugue state most of the time thinking about all the ways he wants to do it to her. So when she says "Hey, daddy, reach me that fruit," he says without thinking, "Sure, baby, whatever you want," and boom, there they go on their midnight ride to Nowheresville. And for all eternity we're not only totally hung up on food, we can never seem to get enough sex, have you noticed that? But I ask you, what woulda happened if Adam had just said, "Bitch, get that fruit outta your head," and decked her, boom. You think we'd be in the mess we're in now? No way. We'd be living in a place that looks a lot like ... *(He looks at the garden and says with feeling.)* Well, a whole hell of a lot like your back yard, Ray. I think it's one of the most beautiful spots on earth.

RAY. Thank you.

WARREN. I mean it.

RAY. Look, for one thing that is not a real story, Adam and Eve.

WARREN. How do you know?

RAY. It's a fable that attempts to explain the genesis of human suffering.

WARREN. Women are the genesis, Raymond!

RAY. You consider the times, Warren, men were trying to stamp out the goddess culture that was six thousand years old, it's pure politics.

WARREN. I don't always trust how you talk, it's not masculine.

RAY. One person cannot be the sole cause of human suffering.

WARREN. Unless they are a woman.

RAY. You've stopped reading and you're watching too much TV.

WARREN. No.

RAY. Yes, you are, because you're talking like an idiot.

WARREN. Have you, Ray, son of God, ever hit your wife?

RAY. I told you ... *(Beat.)* Okay, what do you mean by hit?

WARREN. Punch, slap, kick, shake, trip, pinch, pull, squeeze. Push.

RAY. Okay, I might have pushed her to keep her from hurting herself one time.

WARREN. To keep her from getting hurt you pushed her.

RAY. She was coming at me with a knife and I pushed her away, not hard, just a little shove but we were gassed and I guess she lost her balance and fell into this glass table and that was kind of a mess ... stitches and bleeding and all kinds of dirty looks from nurses at the emergency room wondering if she wanted to call the cops which she did not, of course, since she was, unbeknownst to me at the time, running that credit card scam that eventually got her popped for grand larceny.

WARREN. This happened with Denise?

RAY. No! Not Denise, I wasn't talking about Denise, I was talking about Sharky.

WARREN. Ray, you haven't been married to Sharky in years.

RAY. Seven years, Warren. Seven years and four months.

WARREN. I meant the current Mrs. Potato Head.

RAY. No. I never hit Denise. After Sharky I told myself, never again.

WARREN. What are you saying?

RAY. Sharky drove me nuts, you know that. We used to chase each other around trying to kill each other.

WARREN. You're not in love with Denise like that?

RAY. Correct.

WARREN. *(Amazed.)* You're not?

RAY. Don't sound so surprised, it's not like I don't have feelings for Denise ... but it's more like she's my friend. The sex is friendly sex

... accommodating ... but not impossible to imagine stopping entirely at some point and not missing, and in fact, it's actually been quite awhile now that I think of it, I mean, we sleep in separate rooms, she's there, I'm here.

WARREN. Separate rooms.

RAY. She complained about my snoring so I moved.

WARREN. What about in the beginning? The initial attraction, the courtship, the heavy petting, the public sex...?

RAY. Her body is not ... I don't know, she's not my type. Can I say that...?

WARREN. She's stacked.

RAY. Yeah, but I never liked that big boob thing.

WARREN. I love that.

RAY. And she has a smell about her that's ... I don't know what it is, some kind of skin oil, musk. Look, I don't want to say anything against her, she's one of the finest people I've ever met and I'm glad, no, I'm grateful she's my wife ... really. I mean, when Sharky took off ...

WARREN. She didn't take off, you turned her out.

RAY. I asked her to leave when she told me she was in love with you, Warren!

WARREN. But I had nothing to do with it!

RAY. Warren...?

WARREN. Except for listening to her ... that's all I did, she talked, I listened.

RAY. Well, that was a mistake, okay!

WARREN. See, you are mad!

RAY. No, I mean, listening to women is how you seduce women is to listen and pretend to be interested in what is not too interesting you know that.

WARREN. I was interested because she talked about you.

RAY. Well, you shouldn't have listened!

WARREN. You're my brother, I thought I was helping.

RAY. Oh Warren!

WARREN. Sure, okay, I always had ... you know ...

RAY. A BIG FAT FUCKING THING for her...!

WARREN. Right.

RAY. All I'm saying is that it was stupid. It was stupid of you and

13

that's all. Okay?

WARREN. Oh shit, why do we always ...

RAY. You bring it up because you feel bad, that's why! Look, it's over. You've been married a long time and ...

WARREN. But you hate me ... you hold a grudge.

RAY. What was I saying before we started talking about this?

WARREN. You were telling me how you met Denise.

RAY. Okay. She was working at this bar, by the office ... Why am I telling you this story?

WARREN. I love this story!

RAY. Okay ... it's late afternoon and I'm downtown at The Alibi and it's one of those days I'm getting drunk as shit and she's working there and she tells me, she has a thing for me.

WARREN. That's not how she said it.

RAY. You want to tell this story?

WARREN. She said she had a crush on you.

RAY. Oh right, right, she told me she had a crush on me.

WARREN. (Smiles.) That's cute.

RAY. I didn't really feel the same way but I was so out of it and I felt like there was this hole in my life I had to constantly maneuver around to keep from falling into. You know how people lose people and start over, but I couldn't see my way into that until Denise showed up that night with a casserole, she was wearing a baby-doll nightgown under her coat and she just sort of moved in, you know? Girl moved in. Took over.

WARREN. Baby-doll nightgown.

RAY. Actually it embarrassed me at the time.

WARREN. I know.

RAY. Because you could see her ... everything through it, and it shocked me actually ... made me draw back and I had a hard time uh ... you know ...

WARREN. Performing.

RAY. I had to get used to her ... body, was different, smelled different.

WARREN. Baby-doll nightgown.

RAY. She served dinner in that outfit. Moving around the kitchen, serving dinner with her everything just ... you know, seeing everything! (Beat, smiling.) Sharky'd never do that.

14

WARREN. No, I know, she's a prude.
RAY. *(Annoyed.)* She has a lot of class, Warren. She always carried herself just so. You know? Very particular ... her clothes, just right.
WARREN. Till she lost her figure.
RAY. She let herself go.
WARREN. That's a bit of an understatement.
RAY. She's still the same person. Look, women get heavy when they're happy.
WARREN. And when they're miserable.
RAY. I always thought she was happy.
WARREN. No you didn't.
RAY. *(Beat.)* No, I know.
WARREN. *(Beat.)* Let's talk about Denise.
RAY. Denise is more of a ...
WARREN. Down-home girl ... like the song by The Stones. Remember that? *(Warren briefly hums and dances to his version of "Down Home Girl.")*
RAY. I don't like the images of women The Stones have used in a lot of their music.
WARREN. *(Not listening.)* God, you know...! An action like that, casserole, baby-doll, that would change my life! You know, someone would care about MY needs for a change, I'd be a different man.
RAY. Warren?
WARREN. I never had somebody love me like that! I mean, that's what I envied about you and Sharky is how much Sharky loved you!
RAY. How can you say that to me?!
WARREN. Sharky doesn't love me like that! She never has.
RAY. Look, I'm over this, I am, absolutely, that was then and this is now and I'm happily married to Denise and it's fine, it really is, I'm content!
WARREN. Even when it's bad it's better than dating.
RAY. Ugh. I dated a lot after the split. That was horrible. Picking up some poor woman, going out to dinner, getting stinking drunk and having to call her a cab so I could continue to drink on into the night till I blacked out. I had dates like that with women in the building where I worked, I see them now, we don't speak. They avert their eyes when they see me.
WARREN. I answered an ad in the newspaper.

RAY. An ad?

WARREN. For a date.

RAY. What, a personal ad? When?

WARREN. Just recently.

RAY. You did?

WARREN. But she scared me. I went and looked her over and got scared ... she looked hungry, like she was gonna eat me. Big teeth. Big eyes. Red dress, Ray, have you ever dated a woman in a red dress?

RAY. Could you see her hands?

WARREN. *(Remembering.)* Yes. Yes. They were big.

RAY. Maybe it was a man?

WARREN. Oh shit, I never thought about that ... wow. Hmmm. That's weird. A man. I've never had sex with a man. I mean not in a dating situation ... just, you know, on the job ... workin' vice, but hey, couldn't be worse than no sex ... right?

RAY. Are you dating strangers when you're married?

WARREN. Dating, no. Answering an ad, yes, I did that.

RAY. That's creepy.

WARREN. Right, considering I broke up your marriage, right?

RAY. I don't like to think of it like that, Warren! I just don't ... don't really like to think of it like that, it's not like that, it's, it's something that happened a long time ago to people that no longer exist and nobody can know how these things occur, except sometimes in retrospect, but really, I don't want to know, you know? I just prefer to think it's history and it's nobody's fault.

WARREN. It's my fault.

RAY. Shut up!

WARREN. NO it is and I felt bad BUT then you met Denise and I thought, whoa. Jackpot. You know, with the figure and the baby doll ... but you don't love her!

RAY. Warren ... Denise is great. She is the best.

WARREN. But you don't love her.

RAY. No, no, it's just, she has a few annoying habits that ... look, it's not a problem, I mean, after six years you get used to the way people are, I mean, you endure. Like everything in the house is perfect, not a speck of dust. But look at this place, it's furnished like a cheap motel. And the house stinks, she can't cook a meal

16

without burning something and she won't open a window, so everything I own ... Smell my shirt. *(He puts his arm under Warren's nose ...)*

WARREN. I can't smell anything.

RAY. It reeks of cigarette smoke, burnt food, this perfume she wears and the woman herself! I can't stand to come home sometimes, Warren. The thought of it makes me physically ill. That's why I made the garden, a place to go, a refuge of sorts if you don't have one, if you've lost your place in nature by losing the love of your life you make a habitat where you fantasize day in and day out that maybe someday your Jane will return to her Tarzan.

WARREN. Oh God, Ray.

RAY. It's a joke, Warren, lighten up ... I'm teasing.

WARREN. No you're not.

RAY. *(Weak laugh.)* No, I know. *(Warren and Ray have been drinking all along but Warren definitely takes a drink now. He is stricken.)* Odor is ninety percent of sex, you ever hear that?

WARREN. Only from you.

RAY. When I met Sharky she was a dancer at the Kahala Hilton and we were right up front and she dances by me and the smell of her body was like a sweeter version of my own musk ... I took a deep breath of that and the orchids and the plumeria and I was a lost man.

WARREN. I was sitting right there.

RAY. I felt like the floor was sliding out from under me and I turned and told you I was going to marry her.

WARREN. You were ready. Anyone could have had you. And don't forget about the magic of the islands. I bet if you went back to the Kahala Hilton today, you'd fall in love all over again.

RAY. No, because I took Denise there on our honeymoon and it wasn't the same. It was overrun with show business people and the hotel had put in this aquarium with a dolphin that swam back and forth in this shallow trough where kids or anybody could reach in and touch him and people kept touching him and the animal seemed half mad from all the touching. God! And Denise being fair burned easily and spent all day indoors complaining about how much I was drinking. Maybe we'd been together too long to expect a sense of celebration about our marriage, or maybe it was me, but

I can trace the decline of my life from that trip, the sense of futility, the dolphin trapped in that tank. I got sick off a piece of fish I paid twenty-seven dollars for. Bad fish, in Hawaii, what are the chances of that? *(A long beat, both men seem lost in their own thoughts. Ray rouses himself ...)* So ... what did you two fight about?

WARREN. When?

RAY. Tonight.

WARREN. Oh. You know. Stupid shit.

RAY. Uh huh.

WARREN. *(Sadly.)* Yeah.

RAY. What was it?

WARREN. Coming home early, she came home early.

RAY. Home early is the problem?

WARREN. I don't always like being around other people. You know? Just the sound of people moving around the house, scraping chairs, the refrigerator opening and closing a million times, I guess I was just in that kind of mood.

RAY. Well, shit, Warren, she lives there.

WARREN. Well, shit, Ray, if you're gonna be on her side.

RAY. I'm just saying that she is living there, she is paying half of everything, right?

WARREN. More than half since I got demoted and I work regular hours, no overtime.

RAY. It was not a demotion, the evidence room is a very big responsibility.

WARREN. I was a detective, Ray, I was in line for a promotion.

RAY. What difference does it make ... you'll still get your pension.

WARREN. I don't look at retirement the same way you do. I liked my job. I was a good cop, that's all I ever wanted to be.

RAY. But you blew it.

WARREN. What would you do if you were disappointed in love?

RAY. Get a divorce.

WARREN. I couldn't do that to you! Break up your home and then just bail. I had an obligation to stick it out.

RAY. You didn't do this for me!

WARREN. Yes, of course for you, but man, I was so miserable ... that's when I started using ...

RAY. Look, the material point is, Sharky helps with the bills, she

18

has the right to come home when she likes.

WARREN. I know but what about my rights? I had things I needed to do ... I ASKED HER, what are you gonna do today? And she says, I'll be gone all day. And then cool as a breeze she blows back in early, surprises the hell out of me and then she gets mad and I get mad because I think, frankly, she was checkin' up on me to make sure everything was ... you know ...

RAY. You were being good.

WARREN. If I WANTED to get high I don't even know where I'd go anymore.

RAY. So what were you doing when she got mad?

WARREN. Well, you know, whatnot.

RAY. What's whatnot?

WARREN. This and that, this and that.

RAY. Warren?

WARREN. Well, art projects. Okay?

RAY. Art projects?

WARREN. Yes and she came in on me while I was doing them and started screaming and ...

RAY. What were you doing that would make her scream?

WARREN. I told you, art projects.

RAY. What do you mean by art projects?

WARREN. Why do you say it like that, I went to college.

RAY. Just tell me what that means?

WARREN. I take photographs.

RAY. I NEVER knew that.

WARREN. Now you do, big deal ...

RAY. When did you start doing this?

WARREN. I don't know ... awhile ago.

RAY. So Sharky was screaming at you for taking art photos.

WARREN. She got hysterical and was gonna call the cops.

RAY. The cops?

WARREN. Hysterical, you know how she gets.

RAY. What were you taking a picture of exactly?

WARREN. Nothing.

RAY. Warren?

WARREN. What difference does it make? It was an artistic statement.

RAY. I want to know what she saw that made her scream?

WARREN. It was a still life.

RAY. Like … fruit, flowers, dead birds?

WARREN. My neighbor's daughter, she wants to be a model and so I took some pictures of her as a favor to help her get started.

RAY. Pictures of your neighbor's daughter.

WARREN. Polaroids. That's how you do it, before you waste the film you take a few Polaroids. Because for one thing I don't actually have a good camera yet but these Polaroids are not cheap, the film's like twenty bucks.

RAY. How old is the girl, Warren?

WARREN. I don't know.

RAY. Yes you do too.

WARREN. Sixteen.

RAY. Shit!

WARREN. I was trying to help her out, help her get started. Where do you think Marilyn Monroe would be if that calendar guy hadn't taken her picture?

RAY. What was she wearing?

WARREN. Have you ever seen the painting of Venus on the half-shell?

RAY. Warren…?

WARREN. What?

RAY. She was naked?

WARREN. Naked with a very LONG wig!

RAY. And where did you take these pictures?

WARREN. In my studio.

RAY. You mean the basement?

WARREN. If you don't stop sounding like a wife you're gonna have to fuck me and take care of me when I'm old.

RAY. That may happen anyway. So, you're taking nude photos of a sixteen-year-old girl in your basement, Warren, and Sharky came in on you and you're mad at HER?

WARREN. Art is a process, you know … it's personal, she didn't understand, she just got mad …

RAY. Can you blame her?

WARREN. I was doing a favor for a friend.

RAY. Warren, I'm looking right at you, I can see you, I can see inside you, I can see you had a thing for this girl.

WARREN. She's like a ripe fruit.

RAY. She's fourteen.

WARREN. This kid is very mature for her age, she has womanly ways.

RAY. Warren, she's a baby.

WARREN. You don't know these girls nowadays, man, they grow up fast what with MTV and all kinds of sexy talk in the school yard and these movies, all kinds of movies about sex and longing and the unfulfilled promise of love, and they can't say NO, they don't have language, the schools don't encourage debate so you can do what you like as long as YOU keep talking and it doesn't hurt them and you know they all want to be models so they can be wanted by millions of lonely men humping their mattresses in the middle of the night, jerking off to these images in their heads while their wives make up stories about how THEY can't have sex tonight. Bleeding, gas, imaginary pains, and if I complain it's always about what's wrong with ME. I'm selfish because I wake her up when the bed starts shaking because I have to relieve myself manually, and she is disgusted and starts screaming and it makes you want to kill these goddamned women when they lose their love for you and all they want to do is use you for a paycheck and complain to their friends about what kind of animal in heat you've turned out to be and how it's all gotten worse as you've gotten older and uglier and all the time they're keeping this precious thing you need so deep inside themselves, so hidden, they keep it deep inside where you need to be, but they won't let you back in there, they can't let you in because of something that happened, you don't know what it is, it's a mystery, they won't talk to you about it and you ask them what's wrong and they say nothing, nothing, nothing and meanwhile you're dying of loneliness because it's lonely out here …

RAY. Take it easy …

WARREN. It's a lonely fuckin' planet, Ray, and everybody is just walking around like it's all okay and it's not, it's not … it's fucked up.

RAY. *(Beat.)* So how's it stand with Sharky?

WARREN. Pretty raw.

RAY. Right.

WARREN. It's not ... it's not good, Ray.

RAY. Why didn't you say something?

WARREN. What am I supposed to say? OUCH?

RAY. I don't know but they say talking helps.

WARREN. Women say it 'cause they like to talk you into things but you wouldn't know that because you're not married!

RAY. Yes I am.

WARREN. No! Not really. I found that out tonight. You're not! Not like I am, I'm married! Even now, there is a shred of something akin to passion that runs like a golden thread through the tapestry of my hatred!

RAY. You should get a divorce, Warren.

WARREN. Easy for you to say.

RAY. I'm telling you as a brother who loves you, you are too miserable. Your misery is eating you up and spitting out an entirely different person.

WARREN. Don't you miss being married...?

RAY. I am married!

WARREN. The arguing, the sex, the food, the bathroom smells, the inconvenience of emotion...?!

RAY. Warren, there are other ways to be married ...

WARREN. What do you think the five senses are for?!

RAY. To keep you from bumping into things.

WARREN. They are to hear, to see, to touch, to smell and to taste the flesh of another human being! *(Ray diagnoses Warren's zeal partly as an avoidance tactic.)*

RAY. You didn't eat today, did you?

WARREN. These senses locate you, Ray, they put you in the world, they place you on the earth, in all its glory and horror, right here! Feeling, inhaling and touching yourself, alive in this flesh-and-blood lifetime ...

RAY. *(Exiting to the kitchen.)* You didn't eat and you're drinking!

WARREN. Animal in the dirt, rolling in the dirt...! Groveling at the feet of the goddess!

RAY. *(Off.)* I'm making you something to eat ...

WARREN. You can't even hear what I'm saying, but I'm throwing you a lifeline, I'm talking about what makes it real with another human being is sex and emotion and intimacy, Ray, intimacy, is what we need, knowledge of the other, deep heartfelt knowledge of yourself, of another person, of several people...! *(Beat.)* You ever go to a swap party, Ray?

RAY. *(Enters.)* It's not my thing. *(Ray comes back with a tin of sardines, crackers and a glass of orange juice. He hands the juice to Warren who drinks it. Ray opens the tin and fixes Warren a cracker with fish on it.)*

WARREN. *(Calming.)* Sex is what the senses are for ... if you don't have that, what have you got?

RAY. Well, for one thing, control. Okay? I'm not like you, I'm not out of control. That's what I couldn't stand about being married to Sharky. That feeling of being out of control, after awhile it's too much. And look at you, you're outta control.

WARREN. But that's what marriage is for, it's to keep us from getting lost in our animal ... letting our animal run us around this lonely planet, Ray. Women are supposed to be the watchdogs and the saviors. I know that now. Now that I am cast adrift in this wasteland. Sharky saved you but she couldn't save me. *(Larry appears in the garden. Ray sees him.)*

RAY. Oh shit.

WARREN. *(Looking.)* Who is it? *(The men watch as Larry lets himself in the sliding glass door. The three men watch each other for a long beat.)*

LARRY. Hi, Ray. What're you doin'? Havin' a party? A boy party?

RAY. This is my brother Warren. *(Ray and Warren watch Larry. The men do not shake hands. Larry is like a visitor from another planet. He speaks carefully but not slowly. He never looks at Ray or Warren unless indicated. He moves or looks around the room as he speaks.)*

LARRY. Warren, Larry ... glad to meet you. So you're Ray's brother. That's nice. To have a brother. How you doin', Ray?

RAY. I'm good.

LARRY. That's not what I hear. I hear you suck.

WARREN. *(To Ray.)* Should I leave...?

RAY. No!

LARRY. No, stay here. You stay where you are. *(To Ray.)* Don't you love that, the respect of men for other men's privacy, that is so important, women never understand that, do they? They are too

23

curious. Not that I'm not a curious person. But mostly about real things. Three-dimensional objects as opposed to feelings. I don't really have feelings, but I do have hobbies.

WARREN. I have a hobby.

LARRY. What is your hobby?

WARREN. Photography. Artistic photography.

LARRY. I study anatomy. It's a most useful science in my line of work. To know exactly how to separate a joint, pop, where to apply the pressure, crack, where to make an incision. *(Sound.)* The mess you can avoid with a little education.

WARREN. *(With intention.)* Ray loved school, he's a lawyer, I hated school, I'm a cop.

LARRY. Not anymore. Now you're a clerk.

WARREN. *(To Ray.)* How does he know that?

RAY. I don't know.

LARRY. It's because I'm in the know. I bet I know more about you two than each of you knows about each other.

WARREN. That would surprise me.

LARRY. Why?

WARREN. Because I am a student of human nature and my brother is one of my favorite subjects.

LARRY. Because you love him.

WARREN. I guess that's right.

LARRY. Emotional attraction. I don't feel that. In here, where feelings are supposed to live there is a void. Calm and cold. *(Larry pulls a collarbone out of his pocket.)* Ever see one of these?

WARREN. It's a bone.

LARRY. It's a clavicle or collarbone of a sixty-four-year-old used car salesman in Vegas, washed up on his luck. The trick is to take the bone while the guy is alive. They scream like babies, these old men, you wouldn't believe it. Then they pass out and wake up, this area around the chest is all caved in … it's just impossible to imagine the pain and you can't move without screaming in agony and then they put this prosthetic piece in there that never sits right. There's a clicking sound every time you take a breath just so you never forget what a loser you are. *(Larry moves to the door.)* However. This is not your fate. Clavicle. No sir. Our mutual acquaintances have instructed me to prepare a very special treat for you. So. I'll be seein' you Ray. Not now, but soon. By the light of the moon. *(Howls. Larry exits.)*

WARREN. Eeeeyuck. *(Grimacing.)* Who is that guy?

RAY. Who do you think he is, he's a collector, he collects bones … you've never heard of Bone Daddy?

WARREN. Bone Daddy … THE Bone Daddy?

RAY. Exactly.

WARREN. How did you meet him?

RAY. How do you think? I made a bad loan.

WARREN. Ray … from maniacs you borrowed money?

RAY. I met them through my bookie.

WARREN. What bookie?

RAY. My bookie!

WARREN. You have a bookie?

RAY. Just for football games, fights.

WARREN. You bet on fights and football games with a bookie?

RAY. And the dogs.

WARREN. You bet the dog races with a bookie?

RAY. Why do you say it like that, it's no big deal.

WARREN. How much are you in for?

RAY. Twenty.

WARREN. Oh man! Have you told Denise?

RAY. Of course not.

WARREN. She's got savings.

RAY. I know that.

WARREN. Maybe if you tell her about Bone Daddy?

RAY. Are you nuts? If I get the money from Denise I'll never hear the end of it. If I tell her why I need it I'll become a prisoner, I'll never be able to go anywhere or make a phone call. *(Mocking voice.)* Where're you goin', who're you callin', your bookie?

WARREN. How were you planning on handling it?

RAY. I was planning on ignoring the problem and hoping it would go away. *(Ray pours more drinks.)*

WARREN. Yeah … that works just often enough to make it a viable option for guys like us.

RAY. What do you mean, guys like us?

WARREN. Guys like us on the outside of the action.

RAY. I don't know if I'd put it that way, Warren.

WARREN. Oh, but that's how it is. We took a wrong turn and we end up here, sitting here, talking about the past, about what's happening now, each fresh disaster, pretending they don't have a thing in the world to do with each other.

RAY. They don't.

WARREN. Sure they do, because you and me, brother, we got off the train.

RAY. What train?

WARREN. It's the path you were born to follow but you got off because you got scared, you couldn't see into the tunnel, you had no faith that there was a light up ahead and in the darkness you panicked and jumped off and started running and you've been running ever since.

RAY. Okay, look, I CAN … get … the money … from Denise, I don't want to do it but I CAN do it.

WARREN. It's not about the money, Ray. You should never have split with Sharky.

RAY. *(Beat, incredulous.)* Warren?

WARREN. That was your mistake.

RAY. She left me for you! SHE left ME!

WARREN. She would have come back eventually. They always do. A woman loves like that once in a lifetime. You shoulda followed your heart.

RAY. You're a sick man, Warren.

WARREN. If you had you wouldn't be in trouble with these maniacs. You gamble because you got off the train.

RAY. Look, I used to go to Vegas and win, asshole.

WARREN. When you were married to Sharky.

RAY. I'm gonna have to kill you now…! *(Ray starts for Warren, Warren ducks him, outmaneuvers him, they chase each other around the room.)*

WARREN. You had phenomenal luck.

RAY. If you come here and let me get a grip on your neck, I swear it'll be quick.

WARREN. Well, it's true.

RAY. One good twist.

WARREN. Don't you remember?

RAY. Come here I said!

WARREN. Wait, what's that…? *(The sound of a key in the lock, Denise is home. Ray starts to take the food back to the kitchen, Warren takes the tray and heads out the garden door, Ray hurriedly straightens up and flops down on the couch, feigning sleep. Denise enters, kisses him, starts off, stops, sensing something, turns, looks at him.)*

DENISE. What's the matter with you?

RAY. When?

DENISE. Now.

RAY. I'm fine.

DENISE. You look weird.

RAY. No. I'm fine, I'm just … well … okay, sit down.

DENISE. No.

RAY. I need to talk to you.

DENISE. Can't it wait, it's close to midnight.

RAY. I'd prefer to discuss this with you now, otherwise, I won't be able to sleep?

DENISE. What about my sleep? What if what you're going to discuss with me is going to sicken me and cause me to be unable to sleep.

RAY. Has that ever happened…?

DENISE. Yes.

RAY. When?

DENISE. The time you slept with my sister and you were drunk and decided full disclosure was …

RAY. Okay, fine, we'll talk in the morning. Jesus!

DENISE. What, you sleep with somebody?

RAY. God … No!

DENISE. You sure, because you look very similar …

RAY. No, it's nothing like that.

DENISE. Oh, well, now I'm all curiosity. Let's talk.

RAY. It's not that big a deal. Well, actually I guess it is. I'm in some trouble, financial trouble.

DENISE. Shit. *(Beat.)* How much?

RAY. About … thirty thousand dollars.

DENISE. Jesus, screw you! What happened?

RAY. I've been playing cards.

DENISE. And you lost thirty thousand dollars?

RAY. I had a bad year.

DENISE. How could you keep a secret like this?

RAY. I didn't want to worry you.

DENISE. You go to that card joint like once a week. Right?

RAY. More than that.

DENISE. Talk to me.

RAY. Other times, I go other times.

DENISE. When?

RAY. I can't remember.

DENISE. Like when I work?

RAY. I guess.

DENISE. Every night when I work?!

RAY. Possibly.

DENISE. And when else, like when my mom was dying and I had to go stay with her?

RAY. You know from that incident with your sister that I don't do that well when I'm left alone too much, Denise. You know that. I eat out every night, greasy food, indigestion, can't sleep, TV sucks, and I don't want to screw up again so I go out and ...

DENISE. Just tell me about gambling!

RAY. I'm telling you how it happens!

DENISE. Like when you say you're going to see so and so and you come home late and make an excuse, are you really sitting someplace gambling?

RAY. I don't know.

DENISE. Tell me if you lied in order to gamble.

RAY. *(Screaming.)* I DON'T REMEMBER I WENT A LOT, THAT'S ALL!

DENISE. *(Warning.)* Don't scream at me.

RAY. Sorry. Okay. Anyway. I now have this collector who is working for these maniacs from whom I borrowed money to pay my bookie ...

DENISE. You have a bookie?

RAY. And he's talking very seriously about repayment. Or else.

DENISE. When you say he's talking seriously what does that mean?

RAY. That he's serious ... it's a business with him.

DENISE. And this means what?

RAY. You know. Bad stuff.

DENISE. I don't know what you're talking about and you won't be clear and it makes me think you're lying again ...

RAY. I'm not lying! Okay? Christ!

DENISE. Then what does it mean when you say he's serious?

RAY. That he'll like hurt me.

DENISE. How?

RAY. He takes bones from people's bodies, okay?

DENISE. Do the police know about this guy?

RAY. I don't know!

DENISE. 'Cause that is illegal. I'm no expert, but that sounds like it might be illegal.

RAY. *(Ironic.)* Really?

DENISE. Yes. So is loan sharking. Being an officer of the court I'm surprised you don't know that. You can call the police, Ray, you could call your brother.

RAY. Oh God ... Denise?! No. Okay? That's not what's going to happen here, alright ... this guy, is like ... he's like, a force of nature, nobody deals with him because he's what he is ... he's outside the law. There's a law for people like you and me but not for me any-more because I've gone outside the law, okay? Now I'm on the out-side of the law, something that most people won't even admit exists, and I'm out here with a psychopath named Bone Daddy.

DENISE. *(Beat.)* Bone Daddy?

RAY. Yes.

DENISE. You want me to take my savings out of the bank and give it to a man named Bone Daddy?

RAY. I know it sounds nutty.

DENISE. The secret world of men and their games, that's all this is, scary talk about monsters ... you boys, when will you grow up?!

RAY. Denise, this is not a joke! I gotta get some goddamned money! Now, I know you got money when your mom died, and I need that money.

DENISE. That money is for our old age.

RAY. I won't have an old age if you don't help me out.

DENISE. It's not just my mom's money, it's mine. I worked for that money at jobs I don't particularly like and now I'm supposed to just give that money up because you like to gamble. You don't get it, thirty grand will clean me out, I won't have anything left. I'll have worked and worked and have nothing to show for it.

RAY. And what would you have otherwise … a condo in Florida? You hate Florida!

DENISE. You hate Florida! But that is not the point. The point is to have a dream. Something that gets you through the day. That gets you through the "Yes ma'am" and "No sir" and "Can I get you another drink" and the car breaks down and you're tired all the time and you don't have sex anymore …

RAY. What about my dream?

DENISE. This is why we haven't been making love, isn't it?

RAY. What are you talking about?

DENISE. You're losing your juice in these joints!

RAY. *(Distasteful.)* Denise…?

DENISE. That's why you can't get it up!

RAY. I hate that kind of talk. You're a beautiful woman but sometimes you open your mouth and it just … it shatters the illusion.

DENISE. Oh, I suppose you want me to act all genteel and feminine but that's not me, money means something to me because I have a work ethic! I come from a blue-collar family, a working-class family, I didn't grow up in Rolling fucking Hills, I didn't go to a prep school …

RAY. Oh no, can't we please not do this lecture, I have heard this lecture, I have heard it, I don't need to hear it now, I really don't…!

DENISE. NO! We can't! We can't do anything you want.

RAY. Look, I'm gonna go back to work for the city and I'll have regular money again. My private practice would be okay if could get it started but I can't so …

DENISE. Why don't you try going to the office once in a while?

RAY. Oh God, screw off … I do go …

DENISE. You're never there.

RAY. How do you know, are you spying on me?

DENISE. I drive by sometimes to see if you want to have lunch before I go to work and you're never there and then I call you up and it's always the machine. What are you, screening?

RAY. Sometimes I'm at the courthouse trying to get clients.

DENISE. Ray?

RAY. What?

DENISE. You're not at the courthouse.

RAY. If I say I am, then I am.

DENISE. No, you're not, you're gambling.

RAY. Not every day, I didn't go every day, some days I went to the courthouse, some days, I was there trying to get clients.

DENISE. Ray?

RAY. I was!

DENISE. Look. I know you didn't try and get clients at the courthouse. That's not you.

RAY. You don't trust me.

DENISE. How can I trust you when you lie?

RAY. Of course I lie, if I told you the truth I'd have no freedom.

DENISE. Freedom for what? For gambling? *(He wants to hit her, he growls in frustration. A moment ...)*

RAY. Do you understand that I was gambling so WE could have a better life, something YOU want ...

DENISE. I want?

RAY. Yes!

DENISE. Everyone wants a better life.

RAY. I don't want it.

DENISE. You don't want a better life?

RAY. I don't even know what that is!

DENISE. How can you say that?

RAY. Because if you really stop and think about it, what is a better life? It's stuff. It's cars and houses and vacations and insurance premiums and working yourself into an early grave for a big empty pile of shit.

DENISE. Cars, houses and vacations are regular life, not a better life.

RAY. So what's a better life?

DENISE. Time and money. If you have a better life you have time and money.

RAY. I was still following your lead.

DENISE. My lead?

RAY. Yes! Because you have unrealistic expectations of success!

DENISE. I do? I'm a waitress!

RAY. You have unrealistic expectations of my success, mine!

DENISE. Well, okay ... I did expect that you'd do better than you have.

RAY. SEE?

31

DENISE. But so did you.

RAY. At first I did but then I didn't! How could I? I was working as a public defender. Okay!? I might have thought I was going to build some kind of reputation for myself. Bringing rich man's justice to the poor. But I was overwhelmed after the first year. My clients were either stupid, evil, greedy or weak, usually all four. My case load was enormous. The paperwork, the plea bargains, the last-minute deals, the investigating, the postponements, the bail jumpers, the very bad people calling me at home, calling me by my first name. Drug dealers, child molesters, gangsters. Hi, Ray, did we get us a good judge, Ray?! I think I fixed those witnesses, Ray! I got a cut that won't heal, Ray! I think my old lady wants to fuck you, Ray!

DENISE. But that's why you went out on your own, you were sick of your job, and you wanted a change so you made a change.

RAY. For us!

DENISE. No, that was a decision you made for yourself.

RAY. I was doing it for us.

DENISE. No.

RAY. Yes, the job was making me nuts and I thought if I started my own practice I'd be easier to live with, that is something I did for us, we discussed it!

DENISE. You told me you were quitting after you'd already quit. You told me on our honeymoon that you'd resigned.

RAY. Okay, but even my mistakes I made for the sake of our life together.

DENISE. Our life together.

RAY. Denise, you have to think of marriage like a business, we each put something into the business and we take out whatever we need, new shoes and uniform for you, a new desk and chair for me, a car for you, gambling for me ... if you got sick, who'd pay the car payment? The partners. So, who's responsible for my debts?

DENISE. You are because you put YOUR money ...

RAY. MY money is OUR money ...

DENISE. Without asking me, into gambling.

RAY. Oh, now I need your consent.

DENISE. If you're treating it like a joint venture.

RAY. Okay, see! THIS is what I hate about talking to you!

DENISE. You've been gambling and hoping to win so that you could keep gambling, it had nothing to do with me.

RAY. I didn't want you to know how bad things were.

DENISE. You think I didn't know?

RAY. You didn't know that I was having problems with work.

DENISE. Of course I did ... I'm paying the bills.

RAY. Oh great, another version of "I told you so."

DENISE. Well, it was stupid to go out on your own.

RAY. SEE?

DENISE. I said so at the time ... that's not you, you're not a leader, you're a sheep.

RAY. OH GOD! DENISE? *(A moment.)* This is ... damnit, this is, you know ... I just ... this is what's wrong with the whole bloody system of marriage.

DENISE. What? All I said is you're not an ambulance chaser.

RAY. That's not what you said!

DENISE. What did I say?

RAY. You said I was a goddamned sheep!

DENISE. That was just my way of saying you're not an alpha wolf.

RAY. But don't you see that your having this idea about me, about my abilities is part of the problem?

DENISE. Why are you always trying to put it off on somebody else?

RAY. It's a no confidence vote!

DENISE. If you were in your right mind you'd know what I was talking about.

RAY. No I wouldn't.

DENISE. Yes you would.

RAY. You're my mate!

DENISE. Your mate? Like Tarzan and Jane...?

RAY. Yes. It's a primal relationship and your approval has everything to do with my success.

DENISE. We're not talking about success, we're talking about getting by. Barely making it.

RAY. In the beginning when I first went out on my own and I was getting a few cases, not a lot, it would have been nice for you to encourage me ...

DENISE. I did.

RAY. Instead of tearing me down ...

DENISE. I didn't.

RAY. And making jokes.

DENISE. What jokes?

RAY. Like the one about that Mrs. What's-her-name with the bad nose job being able to play it like an ocarina.

DENISE. You didn't even know what an ocarina was.

RAY. What is it?

DENISE. A sweet potato pipe, made out of terra cotta, it's like a flute … *(She laughs.)*

RAY. I don't know what's so funny about it?

DENISE. She had three nostrils, it was funny.

RAY. It wasn't funny to her.

DENISE. That's the last joke I ever made with you because you don't get my jokes, you don't understand my sense of humor.

RAY. What about the fat lady that slipped on the lettuce?

DENISE. I don't remember saying anything about her.

RAY. You said that kind of litigation clogs the courts and the taxpayers are footing the bill. Footing the bill was a joke.

DENISE. No, it wasn't.

RAY. I didn't see the humor.

DENISE. I wasn't making a joke.

RAY. I laughed to be polite.

DENISE. You didn't need to.

RAY. I was trying to be a good sport.

DENISE. That's because you're full of shit.

RAY. I was keeping the peace. That's what a good husband does, he keeps the peace. He lets many things go by, he doesn't take issue.

DENISE. He lies, in other words.

RAY. It's not lying, it's keeping the peace.

DENISE. You're not being honest, you're not being forthcoming.

RAY. What's wrong with having private thoughts?

DENISE. Because that's not intimacy, that's not an intimate relationship. I know I'm not the world's greatest cook or decorator, and maybe I forget to open a window but all you have to do is say something, that's all, I'm not going to get mad. Living together is hard even for people who … people who really love each other, but that's not us, is it?

RAY. Well, we may not be as close as we should be.

DENISE. Yeah, but that's important because you want to trade on an intimate relationship that doesn't exist.

RAY. Trade? What are you saying, we're married.

DENISE. If we were married, really married, you couldn't have lied to me.

RAY. I didn't lie.

DENISE. You weren't honest.

RAY. You're not honest.

DENISE. How am I not honest?

RAY. You don't report all your tips?

DENISE. Do you know why you're doing this?

RAY. Well, if we're being honest, let's be honest.

DENISE. Because you're in a hole and since I'm the only one who seems dumb enough for you to con, you've come to me. You've come to me with all this crap about how I left you alone, I'm not supportive …

RAY. I think we should look at some of these other issues, and see how they contribute to the breakdown in communication.

DENISE. If you were so concerned why didn't you say something before?

RAY. I don't like to make waves but if I'm already at sea …

DENISE. Oh, so this is funny?

RAY. No.

DENISE. That was a joke, you're making a joke.

RAY. Okay, forget it. You don't want to help me, fine! We're strangers who live together, that's all. We don't need each other, we can't rely on each other … SHIT! This is just … *(Punching the air.)* fuckin' unbelievable!

DENISE. *(A long beat.)* So if I give you the money you're just gonna pay these guys and that's the end of it?

RAY. *(Beat, calming.)* That's one possibility. But here's what I was thinking. I could pay off as little as I could, as little as I can get away with, and then invest the rest and use the interest to retire the loan.

DENISE. Invest the rest.

RAY. Yes. Because we're in a recession, it's stupid not to ride the market, we're at the beginning of a bull market and you're keeping it in a savings account and it's stupid, it's a stupid thing to do with money.

DENISE. I'm stupid about money.

RAY. Maybe not stupid just ignorant.

DENISE. Right.

RAY. Okay, I know this sounds like a bad idea because what do I know about investing but I was talkin' to Tank and he was telling me about this investment club that he and Freddy were gonna put together with this bartender that used to work as a broker at Smith Barney and ...

DENISE. Tank was the one that got you into that pyramid scheme.

RAY. We've all grown up a lot since then.

DENISE. It's just more gambling you unlucky son of a bitch.

RAY. *(Beat.)* Wait. Don't call me that. Don't ... take it back.

DENISE. No.

RAY. You take it back or I swear to God ...

DENISE. What are you gonna do, hit me?

RAY. No, see, if you say stuff like "I'm unlucky," it'll wreck my luck, that's the first law of gambling, you watch what you say.

DENISE. You're about to lose a piece of your skeleton over non-payment of gambling debts and you're worried I'M going to queer your LUCK? All you have to do is wake up in the morning and your luck is in the toilet.

RAY. Okay, fine. However you want to run it, Denise. But I'm serious. I need the money. I'm on my knees ...

DENISE. No, you're not. You're waiting to be bailed out. You think I'm going to cave in because I love you and because if our places were reversed you'd help me out.

RAY. That's right, there's another reason, I WOULD help you...!

DENISE. Yeah, but you never have two bucks in your kit, so if our situations were reversed you couldn't help me out. I'd have to let Lothar pull the bones from my body.

RAY. You know, you love to do this, you love this, you love to get me in a corner and beat the shit out of me, well, okay ... okay! Here ... here I am! *(Ray gets down on his knees.)* Look at me!

DENISE. No.

RAY. *(Desperate.)* Look at me! I'm on my knees, for the time being, while I still have knees, but Denny, if I screw up with these monsters, I won't have knees, okay? No knees! Please, I'm scared.

I want to keep my body intact. I need you to help me.

DENISE. *(Beat, looking at him.)* Oh my God.

RAY. What?

DENISE. *(Pause. Amazed.)* It's not enough.

RAY. What? What isn't enough, what … I'm on my knees!

DENISE. I don't love you enough.

RAY. Excuse me?

DENISE. If you'd asked me as a friend it would make more sense. But you asked me as an obligation of marriage and I realized, just this minute … I don't feel that anymore.

RAY. Okay, maybe we should talk in the morning.

DENISE. No, there's no point.

RAY. You're upset, this has been a shock.

DENISE. I don't feel married to you anymore.

RAY. But we're married …

DENISE. Yes, but I don't FEEL it.

RAY. Denise, marriage is a legal commitment, you fuck feelings because feelings come and go like the tides, but a legal obligation remains valid, that is what is meant by "for better or for worse."

DENISE. But it's never gotten better it's only gotten worse and I don't know if it's ever been that great between us, it's been more like a friendship, except you don't really like me …

RAY. That's not true!

DENISE. You don't like to come home.

RAY. Of course I do, it's my home, I come here …

DENISE. No, you don't, you don't like it here, you come in and you sniff the air and you go outside, out to the garden … I can tell you're not happy.

RAY. Where are you getting this stuff?

DENISE. From you. I can tell, you don't like the house, the way I've fixed it up, in fact … I know you're going to get mad about this … because you do every time I bring it up, but … I don't think you ever got over your first wife, I think you're still in love with Sharky.

RAY. Oh STOP IT! Just, I am so SICK of your raging insecurity, how can you keep on like this? It's demented, you know, it's psychotic! I have an enormous amount of feeling for you.

DENISE. Gratitude maybe, but not love … never love.

RAY. Denise …

DENISE. I can't blame you, I forced this marriage. You didn't want to get married. You didn't even want a relationship. You told me that the night I came over in that … trashy lingerie with that stupid casserole. God, I've never been so embarrassed in my life.

RAY. There's no reason, it was great.

DENISE. I scared you to death.

RAY. That's not true.

DENISE. I couldn't help it. I knew we weren't really connecting and I wanted you. I wanted to quit working.

RAY. You did?

DENISE. Yes, I thought maybe we could have a baby…?

RAY. Oh, yeah but …

DENISE. No, I know … but I thought marrying a lawyer …

RAY. Right.

DENISE. But that's not the only reason I married you.

RAY. Well, if it was…?

DENISE. No, it wasn't. I loved you. I loved everything about you. I loved to listen to you talk about your shitty job. I loved how miserable you were. I loved how much you seemed to care about your marriage coming apart, how you felt when your wife left…? I thought if I could make you love me like that … I'd really have something … great. That's where my unrealistic expectations came into it. I just thought we could make each other happy.

RAY. We are happy.

DENISE. No, we're not.

RAY. I am.

DENISE. Ray, it's never been a good fit.

RAY. I've been very happy with you.

DENISE. Ray? Don't you think I can hear it when you lie?

RAY. I'm not lying.

DENISE. Do you really think I'm that stupid?

RAY. Denise, I don't think you're stupid, I think you're very bright.

DENISE. Oh my God.

RAY. What now?

DENISE. You really do think I'm stupid.

RAY. I don't!

DENISE. You were patronizing me.

RAY. No I wasn't. *(Beat.)* Maybe just a little but I do think you're intelligent.

DENISE. See, the problem is I loved you unconditionally. That's why I've let a lot of your lies go by.

RAY. Everybody lies a little.

DENISE. You don't. You lie a lot. But think about this, Ray. Think about all that lying. Don't you ever wonder who really knows you? Who really knows your heart? When you die, who will mourn for you. Who will know you well enough to mourn your loss?

RAY. I'm close to my brother. Sort of.

DENISE. I thought you hadn't spoken to your brother since he sold your car to buy crack.

RAY. All I'm saying is he knows me.

DENISE. He knows all about your gambling?

RAY. *(Beat.)* Yes.

DENISE. So he knew and I didn't?

RAY. It's the kind of thing you tell a brother.

DENISE. I see.

RAY. Look, Denise this is not the time, I'm just, I can't, I will, but not now, okay because you've got to help me out here, I mean, this is a very, very extra serious problem, you know? It's not like a joke, it's like a big deal, a very big, extra big fat deal. I'm in a lot of trouble and I need your help. Do you understand, are you getting that?

DENISE. Yes, I understand that.

RAY. You do?

DENISE. Yes.

RAY. *(Relieved.)* Good. Great. So … okay. You're going to have to go to the bank tomorrow morning, get the cash, has to be cash, and okay, new thing, honesty, it's not thirty thousand, I only need twenty, twenty grand, so okay, we'll go get it and you're right, I'm just gonna pay off this guy, forget the investment scheme, we'll do that some other time, when we're back on our feet financially. You know? So you'll go, or … hey, we'll both go, we'll go early, we'll have a nice breakfast, you know, out somewhere, maybe by the beach and we'll go to the bank and then we'll spend the day together, just the two of us, then I'll get the money, take the money, you can come if you want, we'll go find this guy and pay this debt and we'll be free, we'll make a fresh start. I think this has been good, this talking like this, we should do more of this, you know? *(Beat.)* So, you feel like spending the day together, just the two of us?

DENISE. *(Beat.)* I'm sorry, Ray. *(She watches him a beat, exits; a moment later she enters with her nightgown and toothbrush.)*

RAY. Where are you going?

DENISE. I'm going to a hotel. It was your place when I moved in and I'll move out.

RAY. I thought it was all settled. *(She pauses at the door, gives him a long last look.)*

DENISE. Goodbye, Ray. *(She exits. A moment, Ray is in shock. Warren comes in from the garden.)*

WARREN. Wow. That was like watching a big boat sink. *(Warren makes them both drinks.)* You think maybe she has somebody…? Just my observation with women is they walk out very easily when they've got somebody in their head, you know? Like when Sharky left you it was because I was in her head. You know? She had a sure thing, somebody she was sure of, so she was able to let you go, just like that … *(Ray groans loudly and lunges at Warren, Warren deftly handles him, takes him down as he screams incoherently.)*

RAY. AHHHHHAHHAHHHHHHHAHHAHAHHGHHGH-HGHGGHGHHGHGHAHHGAH … *(Warren holds him as he struggles to no avail.)*

WARREN. Breathe, breathe deeply and relax … relax! Come on! Give it up, big boy! Okay! Breathe, now! Come on! *(Warren is stronger and Ray relaxes and lies limply in his brother's arms.)*

RAY. *(A long beat.)* How do you fuck if you don't have a penis?

WARREN. I don't think you do. You can do other things, but fucking is out.

RAY. I've heard of guys thinking they had their legs when their legs had been amputated, swearing they could feel their legs, but what about your dick, what happens?

WARREN. *(Thoughtfully.)* Well, it depends, I suppose on if they just take the dick.

RAY. Right. They could take the balls. I'd have no fluids … what do you think would happen … would my voice get higher…?

WARREN. Stop it.

RAY. Seriously.

WARREN. It's not productive.

RAY. Will I be able to stop shaving?

WARREN. What are you doing?

RAY. Trying to look on the bright side.

WARREN. You know what you need? You need a job. Men need to work.

RAY. Maybe if they cut off my dick I could become a woman ... get married. I wouldn't be able to have kids, the guy would have to love me for myself. Did you ever see *Some Like it Hot*? Jack Lemmon dresses as a woman and by the end of the movie it looks like he's going to make a very good marriage to a millionaire played by Joe E. Brown. *(Warren begins hunting around for the check Ray hid earlier.)*

WARREN. Look, all you need is one good case and you'd be clear of debt. What about this guy tonight ... why don't you just take his case ... this guy that was here with that ...

RAY. Psychotic gumdrop. *(Warren finds the check.)*

WARREN. Look, here's this guy's check for ... Fifty thousand dollars ...

RAY. Gimme that ...

WARREN. This is a very, very large amount of money. This is way more than you need.

RAY. Warren? *(Warren keeps the check away.)*

WARREN. Rich people and their justice, Ray. It's all for sale. What's the case?

RAY. It's none of your business.

WARREN. This girl killed somebody, right?

RAY. I don't remember.

WARREN. What have they got?

RAY. They have a signed confession, they have the knife.

WARREN. Okay, okay ... well, you can get the confession bumped. *(Realizing.)* And I work in the evidence room.

RAY. Yeah, so?

WARREN. It doesn't take a genius to figure out why they chose you, Ray. This guy Larry knows about me, knows about you ... why is that?

RAY. I don't know.

WARREN. It's a set-up.

RAY. What are you talking about?

WARREN. Losing the knife. I can lose the knife. I lose stuff all the time.

RAY. No!

WARREN. Why not?

RAY. No, Warren! An act like this would change everything. It would change our lives in ways we can't even anticipate.

WARREN. Then what difference does it make? We're already off the train, we're already running in the dark ...

RAY. You're talking about cooperating with human evil. That guy is evil, his daughter is damaged.

WARREN. Ray?

RAY. What?

WARREN. Who do we kill when we take a life?

RAY. Did you hear what I said?

WARREN. This is the argument you made against the death penalty and it worked, you got that guy life.

RAY. It doesn't apply here.

WARREN. Come on. Whose life do we take when we take a life?

RAY. *(Sigh.)* We take our own life.

WARREN. That's right. We take a piece of ourselves we've come to hate, we place it out there, on the face of an innocent person, and we murder that person, right? So, who dies?

RAY. Warren, I refuse to become involved in this.

WARREN. The girl was operating at her highest level of good, she was trying to the best of her ability to heal the war within herself by committing a murder, can't you understand that?

RAY. Yes, but it's still murder, Warren.

WARREN. She's a young girl. She made a mistake.

RAY. This is not the first person she's killed.

WARREN. It isn't?

RAY. No!

WARREN. *(Beat.)* Oh.

RAY. For God's sake, Warren, she needs to go away. I know you know this.

WARREN. No, I know.

RAY. I know the one thing we have in common is our love of justice.

WARREN. Okay, so there needs to be some kind of net in place is what you're saying.

RAY. Net?

WARREN. No, okay, I hear you. How about this? What if when she gets out, instead of just walking away she comes to us.

RAY. Us?

WARREN. Or me.

RAY. If she gets off, she'll be free. It's kind of not our problem at that point.

WARREN. But where is the justice in that?

RAY. That's what I'm saying…!

WARREN. But what if when she gets out, we keep her.

RAY. Keep her…?

WARREN. I could keep her.

RAY. You mean, like kidnap her?

WARREN. Incarcerate.

RAY. That's insane.

WARREN. Everyday people slip through the holes in the world because they have failed to learn the lessons of life. Failed to refine their sensibilities. We are neck deep in human excrement wondering where to take our next crap. What is so insane about sequestering a rebellious and murdering girl?

RAY. Well, Warren, it's illegal for one thing.

WARREN. So is murder.

RAY. Warren, what is going on with you?

WARREN. I'll tell you, Ray. Sharky has driven me mad. She has tried to fix what is not broken in me and changed the way I look at myself and now I'm permanently fucked up. What's the little girl's name?

RAY. Vicky.

WARREN. I want to heal my relationship with women through my incarceration of Vicky.

RAY. How did we get here?

WARREN. It's become a two fold plan. I'll lock her up for murder but I'll rehabilitate her for me.

RAY. Will you take pictures of her?

WARREN. If I deem it part of the therapeutic process.

RAY. And for how long will you sequester this rebellious and murdering girl?

WARREN. Seven years, a cycle of time but maybe, if she's amenable, forever.

RAY. Who's going to take care of her again?

WARREN. We will. Or I will. That will be my job. You will have to get some kind of a job and support us. Because I'll be fired, and I'll just stay home. Like a housewife taking care of the kids. She'll be like a daughter to us, you and me.

RAY. Yes, I'm married to my brother, we have one child.

WARREN. Think about it. Wouldn't it be great to have a kid?

RAY. I am thinking about it. Why am I thinking about this? It's crazy …

WARREN. Because crazier things happen all the time.

RAY. It's because I'm afraid.

WARREN. Sure. You're afraid of these evil men that have pulled you into a world of darkness …

RAY. Stop talking for a minute, okay? *(Beat.)* Losing evidence can't be that easy. You will be found out, you will be punished. Right?

WARREN. Right. So … I have to have an excuse. Like drugs. I can be on drugs. Drugs are the obvious choice, especially with a cop like me who has a history of abuse. So, I'll get high and lose the knife.

RAY. And it's just a coincidence you lose the evidence on my case?

WARREN. You don't take the case.

RAY. I don't?

WARREN. Anybody could take the case.

RAY. But I keep the money.

WARREN. You fixed it.

RAY. And you'd do this for me?

WARREN. Yes.

RAY. Why? Why would you do such a thing for me? Give up a job you love, I mean, eventually you would get your old job back.

WARREN. I know that.

RAY. So why would you give that up?

WARREN. You're my brother.

RAY. No. Why really?

WARREN. That's it.

RAY. No, really.

WARREN. I want you to forgive me. For Sharky.

RAY. I have forgiven you, Warren, I couldn't do anything else but forgive you ... I love you.

WARREN. No, you don't understand.

RAY. Tell me.

WARREN. When Sharky came home and started to scream I struck her not in anger so much as surprise. And she fell into the glass door and thrashing to keep from falling ended up cutting herself even worse, in fact, she punctured an artery. *(Ray sits down.)*

RAY. Jesus.

WARREN. She was asking me to help but I couldn't ... I saw what was happening, but I couldn't seem to consider it an emergency. How could I? It was a triumph. I was finally on level ground. She was so weak and pathetic that all my hatred came out and I remained absolutely motionless and watched her dying. Her screaming turn to begging and the begging turn to crying till finally ... and this is how I found out she still loved you ... when she realized she was going to die, she asked me to tell you that she had always loved you, that there was never anyone else in her heart. And then, she apologized to me, she did ... *(Smiles.)* She apologized which I must admit, felt good. That broke the spell, the apology. When she did that I tried to help her, but by then it was too late. She was gone. *(Ray looks around, at loose ends.)* She told me she wasn't trying to fix me, she was trying to make me more like you. Isn't that sweet?

RAY. Where is she?

WARREN. *(Moves to the garden.)* I put her out there. Out there under the plumeria and the gardenia, where the jasmine is in bloom, where the garden smells the sweetest. I put her out there for you. Deep in the rich fragrant earth. She'll be mother to your garden, nurturing it for years to come, if you leave her alone. Can you do that, Ray? Can you let her rest in peace?

RAY. Just like that.

WARREN. We can have a funeral. We just can't invite anybody.

RAY. I thought of her every day, Warren, woke up thinking about her every day. Last thing on my mind at night. First thing in the morning. I still carry her picture in my wallet so when someone I don't know and never expect to see again asks to see a picture of my wife I show them Sharky and pretend we're still married, and that she's at home, waiting for me at home ... the love of my life waiting for me to come home but I can never go home to her now, can I...?

WARREN. Ray, you could have gone home to her anytime. You knew she was unhappy. Why didn't you call her up? One little phone call from you and I'll bet this whole thing, the drugs, the gambling, the human misery, all this could have been avoided. *(A long beat.)*

RAY. Are you ... blaming me?

WARREN. In part.

RAY. Right. Okay. I can see your point. I do see it. *(Beat, he breaks down, gets control.)* But I'm still calling the police on you, you amoral shithead...! *(Ray goes toward the phone, Warren gets there first and takes it away.)*

WARREN. Can I say one more thing?

RAY. Give me the phone!

WARREN. If you leave her there in the garden, she'll always be there to come home to.

RAY. Warren...? *(Warren hands him the phone.)*

WARREN. I know, it's not the happiest ending ... but at least you're together, Ray. It's a way of looking at it, I don't know if you can appreciate the symmetry, but it's there. You have what many people long for with their exes. Closure.

RAY. *(Beat.)* How can you ask me to do this?

WARREN. *(Beat.)* Because we're lost men, Ray. And all we have is each other. *(The two men watch each other. Lights fade. Blackout.)*

End of Play

PROPERTY LIST

Checkbook (ROGER)
Drinks (WARREN, RAY)
Sardines, crackers, glass of orange juice (RAY)
Collarbone (LARRY)
Nightgown and toothbrush (DENISE)
Check (WARREN)
Phone (WARREN)

SOUND EFFECTS

Key in lock

NEW PLAYS

★ **MONTHS ON END by Craig Pospisil.** In comic scenes, one for each month of the year, we follow the intertwined worlds of a circle of friends and family whose lives are poised between happiness and heartbreak. "...a triumph...these twelve vignettes all form crucial pieces in the eternal puzzle known as human relationships, an area in which the playwright displays an assured knowledge that spans deep sorrow to unbounded happiness." *–Ann Arbor News.* "...rings with emotional truth, humor...[an] endearing contemplation on love...entertaining and satisfying." *–Oakland Press.* [5M, 5W] ISBN: 0-8222-1892-5

★ **GOOD THING by Jessica Goldberg.** Brings us into the households of John and Nancy Roy, forty-something high-school guidance counselors whose marriage has been increasingly on the rocks and Dean and Mary, recent graduates struggling to make their way in life. "...a blend of gritty social drama, poetic humor and unsubtle existential contemplation..." *–Variety.* [3M, 3W] ISBN: 0-8222-1869-0

★ **THE DEAD EYE BOY by Angus MacLachlan.** Having fallen in love at their Narcotics Anonymous meeting, Billy and Shirley-Diane are striving to overcome the past together. But their relationship is complicated by the presence of Sorin, Shirley-Diane's fourteen-year-old son, a damaged reminder of her dark past. "...a grim, insightful portrait of an unmoored family..." *–NY Times.* "MacLachlan's play isn't for the squeamish, but then, tragic stories delivered at such an unrelenting fever pitch rarely are." *–Variety.* [1M, 1W, 1 boy] ISBN: 0-8222-1844-5

★ **[SIC] by Melissa James Gibson.** In adjacent apartments three young, ambitious neighbors come together to discuss, flirt, argue, share their dreams and plan their futures with unequal degrees of deep hopefulness and abject despair. "A work...concerned with the sound and power of language..." *–NY Times.* "...a wonderfully original take on urban friendship and the comedy of manners—a *Design for Living* for our times..." *–NY Observer.* [3M, 2W] ISBN: 0-8222-1872-0

★ **LOOKING FOR NORMAL by Jane Anderson.** Roy and Irma's twenty-five-year marriage is thrown into turmoil when Roy confesses that he is actually a woman trapped in a man's body, forcing the couple to wrestle with the meaning of their marriage and the delicate dynamics of family. "Jane Anderson's bittersweet transgender domestic comedy-drama ...is thoughtful and touching and full of wit and wisdom. A real audience pleaser." *–Hollywood Reporter.* [5M, 4W] ISBN: 0-8222-1857-7

★ **ENDPAPERS by Thomas McCormack.** The regal Joshua Maynard, the old and ailing head of a mid-sized, family-owned book-publishing house in New York City, must name a successor. One faction in the house backs a smart, "pragmatic" manager, the other faction a smart, "sensitive" editor and both factions fear what the other's man could do to this house— and to them. "If Kaufman and Hart had undertaken a comedy about the publishing business, they might have written *Endpapers*...a breathlessly fast, funny, and thoughtful comedy ...keeps you amused, guessing, and often surprised...profound in its empathy for the paradoxes of human nature." *–NY Magazine.* [7M, 4W] ISBN: 0-8222-1908-5

★ **THE PAVILION by Craig Wright.** By turns poetic and comic, romantic and philosophical, this play asks old lovers to face the consequences of difficult choices made long ago. "The script's greatest strength lies in the genuineness of its feeling." *–Houston Chronicle.* "Wright's perceptive, gently witty writing makes this familiar situation fresh and thoroughly involving." *–Philadelphia Inquirer.* [2M, 1W (flexible casting)] ISBN: 0-8222-1898-4

DRAMATISTS PLAY SERVICE, INC.
440 Park Avenue South, New York, NY 10016 212-683-8960 Fax 212-213-1539
postmaster@dramatists.com   www.dramatists.com

NEW PLAYS

★ **YELLOWMAN by Dael Orlandersmith.** A multi-character memory play about an African-American woman who dreams of life beyond the confines of her small-town Southern upbringing and the light-skinned man whose fate is tragically intertwined with hers. Finalist for the Pulitzer Prize. "...prophetic and affirmative...a battle cry for humanity and its possibilities." –*NY Times.* "Both a celebration of young love and a harrowing study of smoldering domestic violence, the play is both heartwarming and ultimately heartbreaking." –*Variety.* [1M, 1W] ISBN: 0-8222-1880-1

★ **THE GUYS by Anne Nelson.** Less than two weeks after the events of September 11th, an editor named Joan comes together with a fire captain to help craft eulogies for firemen lost in the attack. Based on a true story. "Ms. Nelson's play...gives credible and powerful voice to a very specific kind of pain...perhaps the keenest message to emerge from *The Guys* is the assertion that writers—and actors—have a serious role to play in a grieving society." –*NY Times.* [1M, 1W] ISBN: 0-8222-1908-6

★ **HEDWIG AND THE ANGRY INCH by John Cameron Mitchell and Stephen Trask.** The story of "internationally ignored song stylist" Hedwig Schmidt, a fourth-wall smashing East German rock 'n' roll goddess who also happens to be the victim of a botched sex-change operation, which has left her with just "an angry inch." "In the whole long, sorry history of rock musicals, *Hedwig and the Angry Inch* is the first one that truly rocks." –*Rolling Stone.* [1M, 1W (flexible casting)] ISBN: 0-8222-1901-8

★ **BOSTON MARRIAGE by David Mamet.** Set in a drawing room, this droll comedy of errors follows two scheming "women of fashion" as they exchange barbs, taunt their Scottish maid and conspire in pursuit of social and sexual conquests as the Victorian era draws to a close. "Devastatingly funny...exceptionally clever...[Mamet] demonstrates anew his technical virtuosity and flexibility." –*NY Times.* "...[a] marriage of glinting period artifice and contemporary frankness." –*Boston Phoenix.* [3W] ISBN: 0-8222-1944-1

★ **THE LIEUTENANT OF INISHMORE by Martin McDonagh.** On a lonely road on the island of Inishmore, someone killed an IRA enforcer's cat. He'll want to know who when he gets back from a stint of torture and chip-shop bombing in Northern Ireland. He loves his cat more than life itself, and someone is going to pay. "...cunningly constructed, deeply and intensely felt, bitterly blood curdling and breathtakingly funny." –*Sunday Times (London).* "The plot is so sublime, the script so witty and the twist at the end so clever that I was won over..." –*The Stage.* [7M, 1W] ISBN: 0-8222-1934-4

★ **THE DAZZLE by Richard Greenberg.** A pair of early twentieth-century bachelor brothers bury themselves under collectibles and trash in their Harlem mansion in this gorgeous tale of mental collapse. Loosely based on the true story of the Collyer brothers. "...a beautiful, disturbing, shockingly funny and profoundly humane play by a masterful dramatist—a writer fearless in his use of poetic imagery, bitterly acid in his irony and, simultaneously, rapturously romantic and horrifyingly clear eyed in his assessment of life." –*Chicago Sun-Times.* [2M, 1W] ISBN: 0-8222-1915-8

★ **BLUE/ORANGE by Joe Penhall.** In a London psychiatric hospital, an enigmatic patient claims to be the son of an exiled African dictator—a story that becomes unnervingly plausible—in this incendiary tale of race, madness and a Darwinian power struggle at the heart of Britain's deteriorating National Health Service. "Exuberant...Penhall has the gift of making serious points in a comic manner and of conveying moral indignation without preaching." –*Guardian (London).* [3M] ISBN: 0-8222-1935-2

DRAMATISTS PLAY SERVICE, INC.
440 Park Avenue South, New York, NY 10016   212-683-8960   Fax 212-213-1539
postmaster@dramatists.com   www.dramatists.com

THE MYSTERY OF ATTRACTION
by Marlane Gomard Meyer

4M, 2W

A darkly comic exploration of that primordial force that makes us slow down at the scene of an accident or eavesdrop on a fight in an adjacent motel room. When Ray, an attorney badly in debt to the wrong people, is offered a lucrative, if repugnant case that will require him to break the law, it precipitates a night in which he and his brother, Warren, discover that their catastrophic life choices have less to do with bad luck and everything to do with the mystery of attraction.

"… sophisticated and ambitious … touching and funny …"
—The New York Times

"… hilariously amusing dialogue …"   **—Curtain Up**

"Rarely have a pair of pathetic, degenerate and whiny losers been so much fun to listen to … a dark, quirky comedy."
—The New York Daily News

Also by Marlane Gomard Meyer
THE CHEMISTRY OF CHANGE
ETTA JENKS

ISBN 0-8222-1947-6

DRAMATISTS PLAY SERVICE, INC.